C000259860

Preface:

About 10 years ago The Holy Spirit started to show me things about Jesus that were very surprising and very exciting. There are many, many things hidden in this story. I personally think that the Lord has hidden a few mysteries to disclose at the right time. I hope this is the right time for you. When I say mystery please understand:

Disclaimer:

There is nothing in here heretical, nothing against the mainstream understanding of the Trinity, nothing in agreement with any cult and nothing that is disputed by any mainstream church. What is contained here is unusual not because it is controversial but just that no one seems to have seen it or discussed it in detail before. Nothing here is essential to salvation and everything here could be disagreed with and there would be no loss of salvation. Please read and tread with love.

For the name of Jesus I am using Yeshua. It is a small thing but if you remember there is no letter J in Hebrew. It is a Y. So Jesus (His name is a translation of course) was in fact named Joshua and Joshua with a Y, or Yeshua (Pronounced a bit like "Yes you are" and a bit like Yoshua). His family would have called Him Yeshua when speaking to Him. Yeshua was born into a deeply religious system that have traced their ancestors back to David and beyond, and was related to serving men in the Temple (ref his cousin's father Zechariah). I can assure you his name was Hebrew. Names matter. Zechariah was actually struck dumb when he argued with the Angel about the name of his son John.

If you ask an average Christian they will be very quick to tell you that Moses did not make it to the Promised Land in the bible. Well that is not strictly true...

Prologue: (From Matthew 17)

"On a mountain somewhere near Galilee in the Promised Land something odd was about to take place. Jesus (Yeshua) had taken three of his disciples and climbed a mountain. What was about to happen would amaze them and leave one of them literally "out of his mind" and "unaware of what he was saying". In front of them two very special events were about to take place. The first event was the Messiah revealing who He really was (transfigured before their eyes)... but the second event would have even deeper significance. Moses was about to reach the Promised Land."

This short book Chronicles the much overlooked Restoration of Moses. Why was he restored and what did he and Yeshua speak about. To our amazement scripture tells us clearly exactly what they discussed.

Scripture is clear Moses has died. His bones were never found but he has died. Elijah has not died. Elijah can visit Earth if so permitted by the Lord however Moses has died. Moses ideally should NOT have been there. Yet there he was. This was the Restoration of Moses.

Lets look into this mystery and unpack what Moses was doing there. First some basics.

Trinity

If you ask any follower of Yeshua they will be quick to tell you that Yeshua has always existed. The New Testament explains who Yeshua is and explains the Trinity. Here we are assuming that you agree with the concept of The Trinity as we will not attempt to prove it in this text, however here is a quick reminder of the relevant texts and verses.

The book of Hebrews is very clear. In Hebrews Paul describes the "Son" as the exact representation of His Being:

> 1 In the past God spoke to our ancestors through the prophets at many times and in various ways, 2 but in these last days he has spoken to us by his Son, whom he appointed heir of all things, and through whom also he made the universe. 3 The Son is the radiance of God's glory and the exact representation of his being, sustaining all things by his powerful word. After he had provided purification for sins, he sat down at the right hand of the Majesty in heaven.

The Apostle John is also very clear.

1 In the beginning was the Word, and the Word was with God, and the Word was God. 2 He was in the beginning with God. 3 All things came into being through Him, and apart from Him nothing came into being that has come into being. – John 1 vs 1-3

In fact our very understanding of the Trinity is based upon Yeshua Father and Holy Spirit and Their combined presence all through time and scripture. We do not have an angry Old Testament God and a nice New Testament Yeshua. We have a Trinity that runs through both the Old and the New Testament with the cross at the rotation point in History.

So. Lets look deeper. If He (Yeshua) was there in the beginning, (before being born) then there would be more scriptures for us to find of the Lord appearing in the Old testament, and of course there are scriptures in both the Old and New testament explaining this.

Chapter 1 - Messiah in the Old Testament

This first chapter covers some ground principles needed in understanding the rest of this short book. We will look at some appearances of Yeshua in the Old Testament.

With the understanding that Yeshua was not created and instead was involved in creation himself (before being born as a man) then we can look at Yeshua who has always had some type of 'man' or Angelic form. This leads us to understand His appearances in the Old Testament.

These appearances of Yeshua in the Old Testament can be referred to as a "Theophany". This is standard and completely uncontested doctrine. From the Catholics to the Pentecostals everyone agrees that Yeshua was in and through the Old Testament. All traditional churches are in agreement. Now of course it makes sense for The Lord to appear as a man in the Old Testament. We are of course made in His image and how else would He communicate with us?

As a member of the Trinity then Christians see Yeshua all the way through the Old Testament.

Lets take a closer look. Here is a collection of some of his appearances in the Old Testament which are by no means exclusive. There are literally tens of occurrences where His part of the Trinity seems to suddenly appear.

1. Before The Fall – In the Garden with Adam and Eve

> 8 They heard the sound of the Lord God walking in the garden in the cool of the day - Genesis 3 vs 8

The first could be Adam walking with God in the garden. His literal footsteps could be heard. God had feet. And feelings. In perhaps the saddest chapter of mans history we can see reading through Genesis The Lords slow retraction of His physical presence. From conversations with Adam and Eve, and Cain and Abel to when He has removed his physical presence entirely and men *"started to call on the name of the Lord"* Genesis 4 vs 26

2. Before Noah - Walking with Enoch

> 24 Enoch walked with God; and he was not, for God took him.
> -Genesis 5 vs 24

Enoch leaves quite a mystery. It is not clear how he disappeared or even if he died at all or was just caught up to heaven. We will refer back to Enoch later. Neither he nor Elijah (carried up to heaven) seem to have died at all.

3. With Abraham - The Destruction of Sodom and Gomorrah

In this story 3 strange visitors appear to Abraham. Abraham understands their true identity. This passage is important. We know the story... but did Abraham pray to the Lord to save Sodom? Or did he speak directly to Him...

> 18 *Now the Lord appeared to him by the oaks of Mamre*, while he was sitting at the tent door in the heat of the day. 2 When he lifted up his eyes and looked, behold, *three men were standing opposite him*; and when he saw them, he ran from the tent door to meet them and bowed himself to the earth, 3 and said, "*My Lord, if now I have found favor in Your sight, please do not pass Your servant by*. 4 Please let a little water be brought and wash your feet, and rest yourselves under the tree; 5 and I will bring a piece of bread, that you may refresh yourselves; after that you may go on, since you have visited your servant." And they said, "So do, as you

have said." 6 So Abraham hurried into the tent to Sarah, and said, "Quickly, prepare three measures of fine flour, knead it and make bread cakes." 7 Abraham also ran to the herd, and took a tender and choice calf and gave it to the servant, and he hurried to prepare it. 8 He took curds and milk and the calf which he had prepared, and placed it before them; and he was standing by them under the tree as they ate.

9 Then they said to him, "Where is Sarah your wife?" And he said, "There, in the tent." 10 He said, "I will surely return to you at this time next year; and behold, Sarah your wife will have a son." And Sarah was listening at the tent door, which was behind him. 11 Now Abraham and Sarah were old, advanced in age; Sarah was past childbearing. 12 Sarah laughed to herself, saying, "After I have become old, shall I have pleasure, my lord being old also?" 13 And the Lord said to Abraham, "Why did Sarah laugh, saying, 'Shall I indeed bear a child, when I am so old?' 14 Is anything too difficult for the Lord? At the appointed time I will return to you, at this time next year, and Sarah will have a son." 15 Sarah denied it however, saying, "I did not laugh"; for she was afraid. And He said, "No, but you did laugh."

16 *Then the men rose up from there, and looked down toward Sodom; and Abraham was walking with them to send them off. 17 The Lord said, "Shall I hide from Abraham what I am about to do,* 18 since Abraham will surely become a great and mighty nation, and in him all the nations of the earth will be blessed? 19 For I have chosen him, so that he may command his children and his household after him to keep the way of the Lord by doing righteousness and justice, so that the Lord may bring upon Abraham what He has spoken about him." 20 And the Lord said, "The outcry of Sodom and Gomorrah is indeed great, and their sin is exceedingly grave. 21 I will go down now, and see if they have done entirely according to its outcry, which has come to Me; and if not, I will know."

22 Then *the men* turned away from there and went toward Sodom, *while Abraham was still standing before the Lord. 23 Abraham came near and said, "Will You indeed sweep away the righteous with the wicked?* 24 Suppose there are fifty righteous within the city; will You indeed sweep it away and not spare the place for the sake of the fifty righteous who are in it? 25 Far be it from You to do such a thing, to slay the righteous with the wicked, so that the righteous and the wicked are treated

alike. Far be it from You! *Shall not the Judge of all the earth deal justly?"* 26 *So the Lord said, "If I find in Sodom fifty righteous within the city, then I will spare the whole place on their account."* 27 And Abraham replied, "Now behold, I have ventured to speak to the Lord, although I am but dust and ashes. 28 Suppose the fifty righteous are lacking five, will You destroy the whole city because of five?" And He said, "I will not destroy it if I find forty-five there." 29 He spoke to Him yet again and said, "Suppose forty are found there?" And He said, "I will not do it on account of the forty." 30 Then he said, "Oh may the Lord not be angry, and I shall speak; suppose thirty are found there?" And He said, "I will not do it if I find thirty there." 31 And he said, "Now behold, I have ventured to speak to the Lord; suppose twenty are found there?" And He said, "I will not destroy it on account of the twenty." 32 Then he said, "Oh may the Lord not be angry, and I shall speak only this once; suppose ten are found there?" And He said, "I will not destroy it on account of the ten." 33 *As soon as He had finished speaking to Abraham the Lord departed, and Abraham returned to his place.* 19 Now the *two* angels came to Sodom in the evening as Lot was sitting in the gate of Sodom. – Genesis 18 -19 verse 1

The first verse of Chapter 19 clearly reveals that only **two** of the three men ventured to Sodom and Gomorrah. This matches perfectly with the statement that "**Abraham was still standing before the Lord.** Amazingly Abraham "came near and said.. **Shall not the judge of all the Earth**" Abraham was in no doubt as to whom he was speaking; the judge of all the Earth. And this 'Lord' came looking like a man. What an extraordinary statement.

4. Jacob wrestles face to face with the Lord.

24 Then Jacob was left alone, and **a man** wrestled with him until daybreak. 25 When he saw that he had not prevailed against him, he touched the socket of his thigh; so the socket of Jacob's thigh was dislocated while he wrestled with him. 26 Then he said, "Let me go, for the dawn is breaking." But he said, "I will not let you go unless you bless me." 27 So he said to him, "What is your name?" And he said, "Jacob." 28 He said, **"Your name shall no longer be Jacob, but Israel; for you have striven with God and with men and have prevailed."** 29 Then Jacob asked him and said, **"Please tell me your name."** But he said, **"Why is it that you ask my name?"** And he blessed him there. 30 So Jacob named the place Peniel, for he said, **"I have seen God face to face, yet my life has been preserved.** 31 Now the sun rose upon him

just as he crossed over Penuel, and he was limping on his thigh." Genesis 32 vs 24 - 30

Clearly the 'man' in the passage had the authority to re-name Jacob. In fact he names all of Israel. Jacob himself testifies that *"I have seen God face to face, yet my life has been preserved"* Is not the testimony of the Founding Father of Israel not enough. Looking back it is amazing that The Lord refuses to name himself. As such He is referred to, to this day as "Ha Shem" – Literally "The Name" in Israeli circles.

5. Samson's parents see the Lord and live

In the following passage Sampson's mother is visited by the Angel of the Lord, and she is told she will have a son. The Angel returns after a prayer and refuses to give his name, but asks for a sacrifice for the Lord. He himself takes the sacrifice and Sampson's mother immediately understands that He was The Lord. The passage reveals how Yeshua visits in the Old Testament and is particularly enlightening. It ends with "We have seen God and lived"

> [2] A certain man of Zorah, named Manoah, from the clan of the Danites, had a wife who was childless, unable to give birth. [3] The angel of the Lord appeared to her and said,

"You are barren and childless, but you are going to become pregnant and give birth to a son. **4** Now see to it that you drink no wine or other fermented drink and that you do not eat anything unclean. **5** You will become pregnant and have a son whose head is never to be touched by a razor because the boy is to be a Nazirite, dedicated to God from the womb. He will take the lead in delivering Israel from the hands of the Philistines."

6 Then the woman went to her husband and told him, "A man of God came to me. He looked like an angel of God, very awesome. I didn't ask him where he came from, and he didn't tell me his name. **7** But he said to me, 'You will become pregnant and have a son. Now then, drink no wine or other fermented drink and do not eat anything unclean, because the boy will be a Nazirite of God from the womb until the day of his death.'" **8** Then Manoah prayed to the Lord: "Pardon your servant, Lord. I beg you to let the man of God you sent to us come again to teach us how to bring up the boy who is to be born." **9** God heard Manoah, and the angel of God came again to the woman while she was out in the field; but her husband Manoah was not with her. **10** The woman hurried to tell her husband, "He's here! The man who appeared to me the other day!" **11** Manoah got up and followed his wife. When he came to the man, he said, "Are you the man who talked to my wife?" "I am," he said. **12** So Manoah asked him, "When your words are fulfilled, what is to be the rule that governs the boy's life and work?" **13** The angel of the Lord answered, "Your wife must do all that I have told her. **14** She must not eat anything that comes from the grapevine, nor drink any wine or other fermented drink nor eat anything unclean. She must do everything I have commanded her." **15** Manoah said to the angel of the Lord, "We would like you to stay until we prepare a young goat for you." **16** The angel of the Lord replied, "Even though you detain me, I will not eat any of your food. But if you prepare a burnt offering, offer it to the Lord." (Manoah did not realize that it was the angel of the Lord.) **17** Then Manoah inquired of the angel of the Lord, "What is your name, so that we may honor you when your word comes true?" **18** He replied, "Why do you ask my name? It is beyond understanding.[a]" **19** Then Manoah took a young goat, together with the grain offering, and sacrificed it on a rock to the Lord. And the Lord did an amazing thing while Manoah and his wife watched: **20** As the flameblazed up from the altar toward heaven, the angel of the Lord ascended in the flame. Seeing this, Manoah and his wife fell with their faces to the ground. **21** When the angel of the Lord did not show himself again to Manoah and his wife, Manoah realized that it was the angel of the Lord. [22] "We are doomed to die!" he said to his wife. "We have seen God!" [23] But his wife answered, "If the Lord had meant to kill us, he would not have accepted a burnt offering and grain offering from our hands, nor shown us all these things or now told us this." [24] The woman gave birth to a boy and named him Samson. He grew and the Lord blessed him, [25] and the Spirit of the Lord began to stir him while he was in Mahaneh Dan, between Zorah and Eshtaol.

6. Gideon sees face to face and is allowed to live

In a similar passage Gideon sees the Lord face to face. Again, the Angel reveals who He is by consuming the sacrifice, something no Angel can do. Gideon exclaims "Alas. Sovereign Lord! I have seen the Angel of the Lord face to face"

> When Gideon realized that it was the Angel of the LORD, he said, "Oh no, Lord GOD! I have seen the Angel of the LORD face to face!" 23But the LORD said to him, "Peace be with you. Do not be afraid, for you will not die."

In the Hebrew these passages use the 4-letter name for The Lord with the addition of the word Angel. Amazing passages of scripture. Baruch HaShem.

The Lord speaking to Moses from the burning bush is a classically understood Theophany. (Appearance of God in the Old Testament). However in this occurrence there is a voice, but there is not the body of a man. This is somewhat different. We see that Moses is asked to take of his sandals for his personal safety and also that he hides his face.

As such this Theophany does not seem the same as the others. We will return to the Moses encounters later to examine them.

> 4 When the Lord saw that he turned aside to look, God called to him from the midst of the bush and said, "Moses, Moses!" And he said, "Here I am." 5 Then He said, *"Do not come near here; remove your sandals from your feet, for the place on which you are standing is holy ground."* 6 He said also, "I am the God of your father, the God of Abraham, the God of Isaac, and the God of Jacob." Then Moses hid his face, for he was afraid to look at

God.....13 Then Moses said to God, "Behold, I am going to the sons of Israel, and I will say to them, 'The God of your fathers has sent me to you.' Now they may say to me, 'What is His name?' What shall I say to them?" 14 God said to Moses, "I AM WHO I AM"; and He said, "Thus you shall say to the sons of Israel, 'I AM has sent me to you.'" - Exodus 3 4-6, 13-14

8. The Pillar of Cloud Leading Israel through the Red Sea

There was an Angel of God moving with the cloud. This is worth noting, as The Lord was clear that He himself would be going with them.

19 The angel of God, who had been going before the camp of Israel, moved and went behind them; and the pillar of cloud moved from before them and stood behind them. 20 So it came between the camp of Egypt and the camp of Israel; and there was the cloud along with the darkness, yet it gave light at night. Thus the one did not come near the other all night.

– Exodus 14 verse 19

9. Paul referencing the Rock in the Desert

The Apostle Paul is also very clear that Yeshua was present with the Israelites in the desert. See his letter to the Corinthian church:

> "They drank from the spiritual rock that went with them, and that rock was Christ.' - 1 Cor. 10:4.

10. Moses meets with God face to face Exodus 33 7-11

Finally we come to the visitations that this short manuscript concerns: The Lord meeting with Moses. As we have discovered these fall into two groups. The first group is the appearance of The Lord without a bodily form. These are characterised by fear and danger, and the second group is the appearances where The Lord and Moses speak face to face; "Thus the Lord used to speak to Moses face to face, just as a man speaks to his friend"

> 7 Now Moses used to take the tent and pitch it outside the camp, a good distance from the camp, and he called it the tent of meeting. And everyone who sought the Lord would go out to the tent of meeting which was outside the camp. 8 And it came about, whenever Moses went out to the tent, that all the people would arise and stand, each at the entrance of his tent, and gaze after Moses until he

entered the tent. 9 Whenever Moses entered the tent, the pillar of cloud would descend and stand at the entrance of the tent; and the Lord would speak with Moses. 10 When all the people saw the pillar of cloud standing at the entrance of the tent, all the people would arise and worship, each at the entrance of his tent. 11 ***Thus the Lord used to speak to Moses face to face, just as a man speaks to his friend.*** When Moses returned to the camp, his servant Joshua, the son of Nun, a young man, would not depart from the tent.

These meetings were face to face.

pā·nîm,   'el-   pā·nîm

פָּנִים   אֶל־   פָּנִים

11. You cannot see my face and live Exodus 33 20-24

However here is just five verses later:

17 The Lord said to Moses, "I will also do this thing of which you have spoken; for you have found favor in My sight and I have known you by name." 18 Then Moses said, "I pray You, show me Your glory!" 19 And He said, "I Myself will make all My goodness pass before you, and

will proclaim the name of the Lord before you; and I will be gracious to whom I will be gracious, and will show compassion on whom I will show compassion." 20 But He said, *"You cannot see My face, for no man can see Me and live!"* 21 Then the Lord said, "Behold, there is a place by Me, and you shall stand there on the rock; 22 and it will come about, while My glory is passing by, that I will put you in the cleft of the rock and cover you with My hand until I have passed by. 23 Then I will take My hand away and you shall see My back, but *My face shall not be seen."*

pā·nāy;

פָּנָ֑י

My face

12. The Lord Himself testifies: Numbers 12 verse 8

In addition when defending and supporting Moses before Miriam and Aaron, The Lord Himself testified that with Moses He speaks face to face.

"Hear now My words:

If there is a prophet among you,

I, the Lord, shall make Myself known to him in a vision.

I shall speak with him in a dream.

"Not so, with My servant Moses,

He is faithful in all My household;

With him I speak mouth to mouth,

Even openly, and not in dark sayings,

And he beholds the form of the Lord.

Why then were you not afraid

To speak against My servant, against Moses?"

peh   'el-   peh

פֶּה   אֶל־   פֶּה

Peh el Peh means literally mouth to mouth.

There are many other visitations of note; Joshua also saw an 'Angel' of the Lord and there is also the 4th man in the fire speaking to Shadrak Meschak and Abednego.

Face to Face?

However lets look again. Several of these visitations have created a challenge. How can they be seeing God face to face and allowed to live?

Exodus 33 vs 20

> 20 But He said, "You cannot see My face, for no man can see Me and live!"

So on the one hand we have experiences with seeing The Lord 'face to face' and on the other side we have a statement that says it is impossible.

This apparent contradiction is really explained by the Trinity. We are able through Yeshua's work on the cross to be present and speak with Yeshua as a full representation of The Lord. These visitations are appearances of The Lord Himself in a human form, which is of course Yeshua. Armed with this understanding lets look again at the Moses "face to face" encounters with Jesus.

Chapter 3: The Moses appearances: An extraordinary timeline

What is unique in this series of visitations is the LENGTH of the visitations. It is clear that The Lord spoke with Moses "face to face" in the wilderness tabernacle for up to 40 years. We forget the timeline of relationship that Moses and the Lord were able to enjoy. Has any man had such access? In fact is there anyone who has ever lived who has had such access to Yeshua? The disciples after all were with him just 2 years and his mother 33 years.

This closeness has largely been overlooked by modern Christianity. If Moses is indeed speaking to Yeshua, and we are absolutely sure he is speaking to The Lord and also absolutely sure that he is speaking with a man (face to face), then this changes our whole understanding of Moses and Yeshua.

We fellowship now with the Lord in our hearts and with the Holy Spirit, however Moses had face to face friendship with him for 40 years. Again I repeat that Moses appears to have spent more time with Yeshua than any living man including Peter and the Apostles. He spent more time with Moses than with his family as well. It is quite an extraordinary length of time.

With this background lets look back to the New Testament and the unusual story that has been skimmed over for 2000 years possibly due to anti-semitism and racism. Lets look again because it shows us who Yeshua really is. In fact the Lord has covered and hidden mysteries in this passage.

Chapter 4 The Transfiguration

Lets look again at the New Testament passage normally called the Transfiguration.

There are three accounts of the story in the New Testament. Lets start with the first;

> [28] About eight days after Jesus said this, he took Peter, John and James with him and went up onto a mountain to pray. [29] As he was praying, the appearance of his face changed, and his clothes became as bright as a flash of lightning. [30] Two men, Moses and Elijah, appeared in glorious splendor, talking with Jesus. [31] They spoke about his departure,[a] which he was about to bring to fulfillment at Jerusalem. [32] Peter and his companions were very sleepy, but when they became fully awake, they saw his glory and the two men standing with him. [33] As the men were leaving Jesus, Peter said to him, "Master, it is good for us to be here. Let us put up three shelters—one for you, one for Moses and one for Elijah." (He did not know what he was saying.)
>
> [34] While he was speaking, a cloud appeared and covered them, and they were afraid as they entered the cloud. [35] A voice came from the cloud, saying, "This is my Son, whom

I have chosen; listen to him." [36] When the voice had spoken, they found that Jesus was alone. The disciples kept this to themselves and did not tell anyone at that time what they had seen.

[37] The next day, when they came down from the mountain, a large crowd met him. [38] A man in the crowd called out, "Teacher, I beg you to look at my son, for he is my only child. [39] A spirit seizes him and he suddenly screams; it throws him into convulsions so that he foams at the mouth. It scarcely ever leaves him and is destroying him. [40] I begged your disciples to drive it out, but they could not." [41] "You unbelieving and perverse generation," Jesus replied, "how long shall I stay with you and put up with you? Bring your son here." [42] Even while the boy was coming, the demon threw him to the ground in a convulsion. But Jesus rebuked the impure spirit, healed the boy and gave him back to his father. [43] And they were all amazed at the greatness of God.

Is Elijah allowed to appear at the Transfiguration?

Now we know that in the Old Testament one or possibly two people have not yet died. We are told that Elijah has NOT died, and there is speculation that Enoch has also not died. Enoch is unclear however Elijah is very clear and uncontested.

Elijah has not yet died. He has been taken up to heaven and has not yet tasted death. Let me explain the importance of this. If a dead person was to appear on Earth this would be a terrible sin and not acceptable in the scripture to the Lord. Saints who have passed death are of course alive to the Lord (ref: Jesus stating he is "not a God of the dead but of the living") however they have died and are not allowed back on the Earth in any circumstances except resurrection. However, Elijah is able to return to the Earth if the Lord willed it as he has not died. Scripture is quite clear on this and many Jews are waiting for Elijah's return. Technically and legally Elijah could return.

Is Moses allowed to appear at Transfiguration?

If you remember the story in Exodus; Moses was told by the Lord that he was not allowed to enter into the promised land. He died before entering the land and Joshua allowed the people to enter the land.

However Moses did die. He dies in Moab and the Lord Himself buried him. Scripture is clear that his body has not been found however he died.

5 And Moses the servant of the Lord died there in Moab, as the Lord had said. 6 He buried him[a] in Moab, in the valley opposite Beth Peor, but to this day no one knows where his grave is. 7 Moses was a hundred and twenty years old when he died, yet his eyes were not weak nor his strength gone.

Moses was buried by the Lord Himself

There is understanding that Moses was also healthy when he died. He appears to have had the breath removed from him in a type of reversal of the breath breathed into Adam. Either way he was buried by The Lord Himself.

What happened to Moses body?

Remember in the New Testament letter Jude wrote :

> 9 But even the archangel Michael, when he was disputing with the devil about the body of Moses, did not himself dare to condemn him for slander but said, "The Lord rebuke you!"

Why was the Archangel disputing over the body of Moses? It is clearly in the letter from Jude. We may never know the true reason (there are several suggested) but we do know that there was an argument in Heaven over his body and his body appeared later at the transfiguration!

Chapter 5: The Restoration of Moses

We can see from the Transfiguration that Moses did make it to the promised land. His feet made it to the land. The story appears three times in the gospels and so three witnesses are provided. How could this be? So how did Moses appear with the Lord? It might have even been a resurrection. Moses spirit alone could not return. This would constitute something against the Lord.

This thought (ressurection) actually has scriptural precedent! It is stated clearly in Matthew 27: 52 and 53, that At the cross just days after the Transfiguration event "righteous" men were resurrected, came out of their graves and were seen in Jerusalem! This is a scripture often overlooked.

> 51 At that moment the curtain of the temple was torn in two from top to bottom. The earth shook, the rocks split 52 and the tombs broke open. **The bodies of many holy people who had died were raised to life. 53 They came out of the tombs after Jesus' resurrection and[e] went into the holy city and appeared to many people.**54 When the centurion and those with him who

were guarding Jesus saw the earthquake and all that had happened, they were terrified, and exclaimed, "Surely he was the Son of God!"

⁵⁵ Many women were there, watching from a distance. They had followed Jesus from Galilee to care for his needs. ⁵⁶ Among them were Mary Magdalene, Mary the mother of James and Joseph,[f] and the mother of Zebedee's sons.

Moses bones would initially have lain somewhere outside of the promised land in Moab. Did Messiah temporarily resurrect him, and allow him to see the promised land before Moses was called to Heaven and the Lord went to the cross?

Chapter 6: What did Yeshua and Moses talk about?

There is a second amazing point. What were they discussing? What was Yeshua talking about with Moses? The answer is given in Luke and it is heart wrenching. Sadly Luke 9 tells us Yeshua was discussing his imminent death on the cross.

Luke 9 is very clear. Yeshua was discussing his imminent death with His friend. Moses had spent more time with Yeshua than Peter, or John or any other disciple. Could it be that Yeshua simply wanted to talk to his best friend before He went to the cross?

28 About eight days after Jesus said this, he took Peter, John and James with him and went up onto a mountain to pray. 29 As he was praying, the appearance of his face changed, and his clothes became as bright as a flash of lightning. 30 Two men, Moses and Elijah, appeared in glorious splendor, talking with Jesus. 31 *They spoke about his departure,[a] which he was about to bring to fulfillment at Jerusalem.* 32 Peter and his companions were very sleepy, but when they became fully awake, they saw his glory and the two men standing with

him. ³³ As the men were leaving Jesus, Peter said to him, "Master, it is good for us to be here. Let us put up three shelters—one for you, one for Moses and one for Elijah." (He did not know what he was saying.)

³⁴ While he was speaking, a cloud appeared and covered them, and they were afraid as they entered the cloud. ³⁵ A voice came from the cloud, saying, "This is my Son, whom I have chosen; listen to him." ³⁶ When the voice had spoken, they found that Jesus was alone. The disciples kept this to themselves and did not tell anyone at that time what they had seen.

Time

So Moses was buried in Moab (Jordan) with the Lords own hands. Could it be, that Yeshua buried Moses, left his body in the care of Michael, and his spirit in Heaven, knowing full well that He would resurrect his body to speak with Him before heading to the cross?

Biblical Pattern

Lets recap the two stories; one in the Old Testament and one in the New Testament:

Moses goes up the Mountain to speak to the Lord. After a while the Lord told him that the people were out of control and he needed to return. On return Moses saw their unfaithfulness and was angry.

Now this time Yeshua (perfect lamb of God) is going up the mountain. This time it is Moses and Elijah at the top of the mountain to meet Yeshua. As Yeshua returns He discovers a ministry mess. His team were unable to drive a demon out of a child. His response was "You unbelieving and perverse generation how long must I remain with you? It appears that Yeshua was homesick for heaven and homesick for his friend that He had just left.

Chapter 7: Summary: A Friend of Yeshua

I am a very sad (in a good way) that Yeshua in his wisdom, had Moses be born generations before me, so that Moses could be his best friend back in Exodus. He then knew he would call later on Moses to be his best friend again before His final journey to the cross. What friendship!

When asked about divorce what did Yeshua say? "What did Moses tell you?" Yeshua was not quoting the law. He was asking what his friend had said. Have we missed the importance of Moses?

Have we underestimated the impact of Moses as a friend of Yeshua, and have we underestimated Yeshua's involvement with Moses and the Law.

This subtly changes everything that I know about my Yeshua. My goal is to one day be friends with Yeshua like Moses was friends with Yeshua.

Printed in Great Britain
by Amazon

32345606R00030